10 Steps to Save Your Editor's Sanity

10 Steps to Save Your Editor's Sanity

by Dr. Jenifer Paquette

4 Horsemen
Publications, Inc.

4 Horsemen
Publications, Inc.

Accomplishing
Innovation Press

Published By: Accomplishing Innovation Press an imprint of 4 Horsemen Publications, Inc.

Accomplishing Innovation Press
℅ 4 Horsemen Publications, Inc.
PO Box 419
Sylva, NC 28779
4horsemenpublications.com
info@4horsemenpublications.com

Cover & Typesetting by Autumn Skye
Edited by Laura Mita

Library of Congress Control Number: 2024935573

Paperback ISBN-13: 979-8-8232-0409-5
Ebook ISBN-13: 979-8-8232-0408-8

Dedication

For my fellow editors

Table of Contents

Acknowledgements

Writing a book is hard—believe me, I know! As a writer, I know just how much time and effort and heartache goes into those pages. I also know how easy it would be to finish typing "The End," hit save, and immediately email my book to my editor and let it become someone else's problem for a little while. That said, I also know how much more my editor can do for me if her time is spent actually editing instead of fixing my careless mistakes—things I could easily have fixed on my own if I had just taken the time.

I know you're tired. I know you just want to be finished, but come on—be honest. You want to read it again anyway, don't you? Just once more to fall into the world your words have conjured...? Sit back, enjoy the read, and clean up after yourself as you move along. The more of these things you catch now, the more your editor will be able to really get into the book, polishing things she can't get to amid the clutter. Trust me—it's worth it.

Why should I trust this Dr. Paquette?

Dr. Jenifer Paquette has been editing everything from creative fiction to technical dissertations for over twenty years. As Lead Editor for 4 Horsemen Publications, she loves helping authors polish their prose to a lustrous sheen. She spent decades teaching English in higher education exploring the history of the English language as well as the intricacies of grammar rules (#OxfordComma). When she isn't debating what part of the punctuation gets italics when foreign and English words mix inside dialogue, Dr. Paquette spends her time writing fantasy and paranormal romance novels as JM Paquette. When she isn't writing, she can be found dissecting grammar, defending fantasy, discussing Tolkien, editing books, guest co-hosting the podcast *Drinking with Authors*, reading books with happy endings, and watching Russian dragon shifter movies.

Why would I help my editor? That's their job. I pay them for that part.

You are absolutely right. Editors can do most of this for you.

But you can take pride in knowing how to properly use the tools of your trade, earning the kind of self-confidence that can eventually lead to self-sufficiency.

That said, I'm an editor, and I still use another editor for my own work. I don't see my own errors when I'm writing—I need another set of eyes and a different brain.

We're wordsmiths—we take pride in our words. Knowing more about how they are "supposed" to work can only help us tell our stories more effectively. Readers prefer well-written work. You can have the best story in the world, but if it's poorly written, no one will slog through it to find out! Building skills to improve your work is an important part of being a writer.

Another benefit to self-editing before you hit send is this: If she doesn't have to decipher each sentence for meaning, she can focus on the good stuff, polishing your prose to show its best award-winning smile. She can spend more time and energy on bringing out the best version of your story (instead of focusing on getting the right words in the proper order to convey the idea).

Part One

Start with the Big Picture

Editing can be an overwhelming task, but you can break it into manageable chunks. This first part focuses on your work as a whole. You should start here rather than tweaking individual sentences—why bother fixing up words that you may end up deleting? Get a sense of the whole thing first, and make sure you did what you wanted to do!

Step One

Consider Point of View

First, Stuff You Should Know (a quick review)

1st person singular POV uses the pronouns I, me, my, mine, and myself.

- This POV tells readers that one person is telling the story (implying that the narrator has survived the upcoming trials and lived to tell the tale!). 1st person POV is personal and gives readers a ton of insight into the speaker, but it's also limited to that person's perceptions of the world and may be unreliable at times.

- "The Tell-Tale Heart" by Edgar Allan Poe features a 1st person narrator who reassures readers of his sanity before calmly explaining how he murdered an old man, chopped him up, and buried him beneath the floorboards. *The Hunger Games* by Suzanne Collins tells the story in 1st person with Katniss relating what happens to her, giving the readers a better sense of her emotional state.

1st person plural POV uses the pronouns we, us, our, ours, and ourselves.

- This POV tells readers that a specific group is telling the story (suggesting that at least one member of the group survives to the end of the story). 1st person plural POV gives more credence to the narrative voice because more than one person agrees on the events of the story—making the speakers appear more trustworthy. It's still 1st person though, so imagine how you describe events when you've done something wrong: you likely try to make yourself look better in the details you include or omit—your 1st person narrator does the same thing.

- It's also very easy to slip in and out of plural and singular, so watch your pronouns. If your "I" becomes a "we" in chapter 7, you need to have some explanation for those extra people.

- To see some effective uses of 1st person plural POV, check out "A Rose for Emily" by William Faulkner (warning—the big reveal is gross) or *The Jane Austen Book Club* by Karen Joy Fowler.

2nd person (singular and plural) POV uses the pronouns you, your, yours, yourself, and yourselves.

- This POV includes readers in the narration, so think about how that works for your story. 2nd person can be brilliant for inclusivity (remember how invested you were in those *Choose Your Own Adventure* series?), but it's also easy to toss readers right out of the story if they don't identify with what you've said. For instance, I was totally into the character in Lorrie Moore's "How," but then she said, "You go home and put on some jazz" and I was out. I've never in my life put on jazz (sorry—just not for me!). So, after that, I was an outsider looking into the story through the windows, watching others act out the events.

- Some great examples of 2nd person POV (in addition to Moore) are "Until Gwen" by Dennis Lehane and *Choose Your Own Autobiography* by Neil Patrick Harris (which has a secret page in the middle if you read it straight through like a savage!). (Psst... this book is in 2nd person.)

3rd person (singular and plural) POV uses the pronouns she, her, hers, herself, he, him, his, himself, it, its, itself, they, them, their, and themselves.

- This POV is the most common in fiction and is a standard way to tell a story that readers will expect and understand. 3rd person POV assures readers that they can trust the narration.

- 3rd person can be used in two main ways.

  ○ In limited omniscient POV, or "close third," the narrator reveals all of the thoughts of one main character to readers, a great way to get inside the head of a character, but may lead to "filter" words like "saw," "heard," "thought," "realized," and others that add a layer between the action and the reader, resulting in slower pacing throughout. Some examples of limited omniscient POV are JK Rowling's *Harry Potter and the Sorcerer's Stone* and Ernest Hemingway's "Hills Like White Elephants."

  ○ In omniscient POV, the narrator reveals all of the thoughts of all characters to readers, a great way to cover huge swaths of characters and epic narrative, but an easy path to reader confusion, especially if you "head hop" (move from character to character) without warning. William Faulkner used stream of consciousness with his 3rd person omniscient narrator and modern versions rely on italics to show shifts in character or time. If you don't want those textual clues, pay careful attention to how your narrator tells the story. Effective 3rd person omniscient stories include Tolkien's *Lord of the Rings* and Tolstoy's *War and Peace*.

Step One Homework

1. What POV did you use for your work? Why did you choose that POV? If you don't have a specific reason (even if it's "because romance novels use 1st person"), think about it. Are you satisfied with your POV choice?

2. Tough question time: Would your work be better in another POV? Test: If you question your POV choices, rewrite the first chapter in another POV and send both to your beta readers. They will tell you what works and what doesn't (plus, they will appreciate seeing the story in a new way—just think *Midnight Sun* by Stephenie Meyer)!

3. It's time to work. Open your document and use CTRL F (Command F on a Mac) to highlight each pronoun. Yes, every single pronoun. You don't need to re-read everything—just scan the pages and make sure you were consistent. Did your 1st person narrator slip into 3rd person midway through chapter 12? Did your 3rd person narrator start talking to "you" the reader (and not in the Deadpool 4th wall break way)?

EXTRA! EXTRA!
While we're here...

- Personal possessive pronouns (his, hers, its, theirs) have one job in English—just one thing—and that's to show ownership: his hat, her jacket, their dog. These words are perfectly capable of owning things without any help—and they NEVER need an apostrophe to do their job. The hat is his, the job is hers, the cat is theirs, and the words are ours. (NOT her's, their's, etc.)

- "You're" means "you are." If you can't replace it with "you are," you should use "your."

- "It's" means "it is." If you can't replace it with "it is," you should use "its." (Yes, always.)

- "They're" means "they are." If you can't replace it with "they are," you should use "their" if someone owns it and "there" if you can point to it.

- "There is" a far better way to introduce a sentence than this phrase. This is weak sauce, and super lazy writing (the sarcastic voice in my head always snarks, "Oh, is there, Captain Obvious?").

    - Super Secret You-read-the-fine-print-and-get-your-money's-worth Extra Credit Homework Exercise: CTRL F (Command F on a Mac) for "there is" and "there are." Delete them—whatever comes after is usually the start of the sentence anyway. For example, "There are many flavors of soup in her pantry." Meh. "Her pantry contained many flavors of soup." This second sentence leaves room for expansion—why should I care about this pantry? What is the significance of the soup? The first sentence is an observation; the second leads into a character detail (now I want soup!). Revising this weak sentence construction also forces you to use stronger verbs—always a plus for readers. (I'm not saying you can NEVER use this, but try to have a solid reason for it.)

- Watch out for ambiguous pronouns like this: John told his boss he had a flat tire. Uhh—who has the flat—John or his boss? I can't tell who that "he" refers to. Say "John told his boss, "You have a flat tire" or John told his boss, "I have a flat tire" instead.

  ○ While you're here, it's time to talk about them. Who? I'm actually not sure. Just "Them." The anonymous "they" who do things in sentences without a clear antecedent (the fancy name for the word a pronoun renames). Make sure you have clear pronoun antecedents (listen to Sean Bean!).

Why do you write it like that?

You may have noticed I put certain things in italics and others in quotes. Here's why: I'm an English major, and we use MLA format to style our writing. MLA puts short works (short story titles, poems, songs, TV show episodes, etc.) in quotes and long works (novels, plays, movies, song albums, TV shows, etc.) in italics. And while we're here—whenever I refer to a word as a word, I will put it in quotes to highlight it. If the word is foreign, I will put it in italics.

Extra POV Practice (for the super motivated!)

Exercises: Rewrite each sentence to eliminate any mixed point of view.

1. When Margo married a widower her life became complicated, and you can't help but feel jealous of a deceased wife.

2. When I ran, you would get cramps.

3. The author suggests that the truth is sometimes painful, but telling the truth is better than living a life being someone you are not.

Extra POV Practice Possible Answers

1. When Margo married a widower her life became complicated, and you can't help but feel jealous of a deceased wife.

a. When Margo married a widower, her life became complicated because she couldn't help but feel jealous of a deceased wife.

b. Margo's life got complicated after she married the widower; after all, who wouldn't be jealous of a deceased wife?

c. After Margo married the widower, her jealousy of his deceased wife complicated her life.

2. When I ran, you would get cramps.

a. When I ran, I would get cramps.

b. Running causes cramps in my side.

c. Because I cramp during my runs, I decided to drink more water in preparation.

3. The author suggests that the truth is sometimes painful, but telling the truth is better than living a life being someone you are not.

a. The author suggests that the truth is sometimes painful, but telling the truth is better than living a life as someone else.

b. The story suggests that while the truth is painful, it's better than living as someone else.

Step Two
Fix Pesky Dialogue Formatting Stuff

<u>First, Stuff You Should Know (a quick review)</u>

Editors can tweak your formatting, but it certainly makes it easier when you do some of the work beforehand—especially for dialogue.

Every time a new person speaks, indent on a new line:

> "What are you doing?" Samantha asked.
> "Rearranging matches," Sebastian said, boredom seeping through his voice.
> "Why?" Samantha inquired.
> "I have no idea," Sebastian admitted.

When a character speaks both before and after an interjection, the punctuation should follow like this:

> "You never have any idea," Samantha sneered. "That's why I'm leaving you."
> "You can't leave me," Sebastian replied, "because if you do, who will organize your things?"

If there is more text beyond the conversation, it can stay in the same paragraph:

> Samantha glared at him. "I don't need anyone to organize my things," she snapped. "I was just fine in my organizational skills before you came along. I don't need someone to look after

me like a child." She scanned the library, haughty eyes taking in other annoying details of his obsessive behavior.

"Huh," Sebastian scoffed. "You couldn't tell that from where I was standing, dear." He turned away from his latest project to stare at her. As usual, her clothes were in disarray, her wrinkled pants and untucked shirt almost screaming her need for his guidance. "Come here, Sam. You look a mess."

"You could use a good mess!" Samantha shouted, stalking out of the library.

All periods, commas, question marks, and exclamation points go inside the quotation marks. You should never put "double" "quotation" "marks" next to one another unless you are making a list of quoted items—otherwise, "double quotation marks" around the full sentence or phrase is sufficient.

Review the Rules:

1. If you start a sentence with dialogue, capitalize the first letter of the spoken words, but leave the rest in lowercase (except proper names). Put a comma at the end of the spoken words (inside the quotation marks) if it's not a question or exclamation point.

    "I don't know why you do this to me," Sebastian pondered. He stared at the books lining the walls, face blank while his thoughts raced. "It's only matches," he whispered.

2. If you start with the tagline, you should start the actual spoken words with a capital letter. Put a comma (if it's not a question/exclamation) after the verb and before the first quotation mark.

    Sebastian said, "She'll be back."

3. If you interrupt a complete sentence with a tag, do not capitalize the words after the tag. If you have two separate sentences with a tag ending the first one, capitalize the second sentence.

    "I know she will forgive me," he moaned, "eventually." He glanced at the door, suddenly sure he heard her returning footsteps. "She's coming back," he whispered. "I know it."

4. If the spoken words are not a statement, put the question mark or exclamation point inside the quotation mark (as long as the spoken words are a question/exclamation). If the entire sentence is a question or exclamation, then put the marks outside the quotation mark.

    "Why do I put up with him?" she wondered, staring down the long hallway. "He's such a jerk!" she snapped, hands fisting at her sides. "Those matches," she mused, shaking her head, "make me absolutely crazy." How dare he say she looked "a mess"? "It's only matches" indeed!

5. Unspoken thoughts should be italicized to distinguish them from spoken words.

    Just one more box, Sebastian thought, emptying the matches onto the table.

6. Only spoken words go inside quotation marks—not reported speech.

    I remember when she told me she was leaving me, Sebastian thought, lips pursing as he began lining up the match-sticks. *Perhaps I shouldn't have said, "You look a mess"?*

7. When quoting someone else's words inside a quote, use single quotes.

    "But why would he say 'You look a mess' to me like that?" she wondered, glancing down at her clothing. "I guess I should be glad he didn't say 'You look a "hot" mess' after all."

8. If your character speaks for more than one paragraph (telling a story), don't use end quotation marks until they finish speaking. This means you will not put quotation marks at the end and beginning of each new paragraph.

Step Two Homework

1. Look at your document in multipage view (3 pages per screen) and check your formatting (you can see your indents this way!). Fix weird lines and odd spacing.

2. Zoom in to your document and check your conversations. Did you use double quotes throughout? Did you properly punctuate your taglines (he said, she replied, etc.)? Did you capitalize the right words? Find the start and end of the sentence—if it ends, use a period; if it continues, use a comma before and after the tag.

3. Use CTRL F (Command F on a Mac) to find speech-related words like "said," "answered," "asked," etc. and be sure you have variety. Also, check that questions have question marks and exclamations have exclamation points.

4. Use CTRL F (Command F on a Mac) to find everything spoken by one character. Read everything said by that person and make sure the voice matches the way you imagine the character speaks. Reading all of a person's words in a row will help you spot shifts in formality. This is how you find those "Oh! He would never actually say it that way!" moments. Do this for all of your main characters to maintain consistency.

EXTRA! EXTRA!
While we're here…

- There is nothing wrong with the verb "said." It's fine. Readers appreciate variety, but you don't need to change each tagline and make it fancy. "Said" is perfectly acceptable. As long as readers don't have to count lines to figure out who is speaking (like anything Hemingway wrote), you're good.

- Try not to rely too much on punctuation to show excitement. Use your words instead. Yes, Stephen King says adverbs are the devil, but we can still use them (just not everywhere!).

- Yes, Americans put end punctuation inside quotation marks (unlike the Brits). This means you would say, "I'm feeling quite American in my usage today." Opposed to: "I'm feeling quite British in my usage today". For US publication, commas and periods go inside quotation marks (while semicolons generally go outside). UK publications often put them outside (and also use 'single quotes' instead of "double").

Part Two

Zoom in to examine the Nitty Gritty

It's time to get real. Open your document and prepare to become a Search-and-Replace Expert. CTRL F (Command F on a Mac) is your friend. Use it.

Step Three

Up Your Verb Game

First, Stuff You Should Know

English verbs are a delightful well of history and confusion. There isn't room here to cover it all, but let's hit the stuff that will affect your writing.

Verb Tense

Tense refers to the time period your verb conveys to the reader. Generally speaking, English has present tense (John walks), past tense (John walked), and future tense (John will walk).

Unfortunately, English is not satisfied with a mere three choices for tense, so it also subdivides these into the simple tense (John above), the progressive tense (John is walking, John was walking, John will be walking), the perfect tense (John has walked, John had walked, John will have walked), and the perfect progressive tense (John has been walking, John had been walking, John will have been walking).

You should probably avoid these multi-word verb phrases in your writing—readers can only handle so many helping verbs before they lose the flow. This doesn't even take voice into account, but we'll get to that in a later step.

Consistency in tense is critical—your story is either happening now, or it already happened. Flipping back and forth will make your editor (and your readers) pull their hair out.

Abstract and Concrete Verbs

Some verbs are better than others. Certain verbs convey action while others slow pacing down. Linking verbs like any form of "to be" are weaker connections—is, am, are, was, were, been, and being. Abstract verbs like "got," "get," "went," and "had" will result in multi-word verb phrases that can distract your readers. Instead of saying "John is walking," say "John walks" OR "John walked" or even better "John hurried" or "John pranced" or "John strutted."

Prepositional Phrases

Prepositions are those little words that tell you where something is in relation to something else (in, on, of, to, with, near, by, etc.). They often appear in phrases, more than one word, and they slow down your sentences, especially if you stack them.

For example, "She stood near the door to her office on the second floor of the building." "Near the door," "to her office," "on the second floor," and "of the building" are all prepositional phrases. They literally hang on to your sentence, but they perform none of the grammatical functions of the words. That sentence is simply: she stood. Everything else is extra—and really wordy. Revise to say something like: "She stood before her second-floor office" or "She reached the door to her office, her space quietly stashed on the building's second floor."

Voice: Active and Passive

Voice refers to the action of the sentence. In active voice, the subject affects the object through the verb (John threw the ball). In passive voice, the subject receives the action of the verb (The ball was thrown by John).

Readers generally prefer action in their sentences, and active voice tends to move the events forward. This is not to say that passive voice is bad. It can be incredibly helpful! Consider the difference: "You did not pay the bill" (active) versus "The bill was not paid" (passive). The first is aggressive; the second states a fact without assigning blame. Sometimes, you need to say it like that. Rather than "You didn't do the thing you were supposed to do, Ms. Boss," you can say "The thing you mentioned wasn't done, Ms. Boss." Passive voice does require more words to accomplish the goal though (threw becomes was thrown), and often leads to stacks of prepositional phrases (The car was driven by the chauffeur).

If you aren't sure if your sentence is active or passive, add zombies (or bunnies, if you prefer cuteness)! Add the phrase "by zombies" to the end of the sentence. If it makes sense, it's probably passive voice. For example: The thing you mentioned wasn't done by zombies. The car was driven by bunnies. These use passive voice. You didn't do the thing by zombies. What? Bunnies drove the car by zombies—okay, maybe this one, but this is a whole new meaning—and a different story!

Step Three Homework

1. CTRL F (Command F on a Mac) all of the following verb constructions and replace them with something stronger/more concrete:

   - is/am/was/are/were + ___-ing (was walking, was going, were talking, are standing, etc.). These constructions are often passive voice, especially "was" and "were."

     ○ Tara was talking to her sister.

       ▪ Tara talked to her sister.

   - got + ___ (got stuck, got held up, got mad, got up, etc.)

     ○ Bill got stuck at the store.

       ▪ Bill lost track of time while shopping.

       ▪ Bill waited impatiently in line behind a woman who clearly needed to unburden her soul to the cashier before she paid for her groceries.

   - get + ___ (get up, get going, get to talking, etc.)

     ○ Joe got up in the morning.

       ▪ Joe rose with the dawn.

       ▪ Joe woke feeling refreshed.

   - had + ___ (had seen, had done, had been, had said, etc.)

     ○ Hannah had seen all of the things.

- Hannah's past exposed her to various experiences. (Even this is boring. It is a stronger verb, but it would be better with an example of something specific in place of "various experiences.")

- Hannah's past exposed her to the intricacies of court politics—she'd spent her formative years in a castle where the wrong nod could get her killed.

- went (replace with journeyed, traveled, drove, ventured, etc.)

2. Find the following constructions and replace them with a more effective word:

- would/wouldn't have to be

- were in need of

- is/was going to

- was/wasn't able to

- seemed to be

- no longer able

- letting go of

- had/hadn't been able

3. Find prepositional phrases and see how you can shorten/replace them, especially if you have stacks of them.

EXTRA! EXTRA!
While we're here…

- Keep genre expectations in mind when choosing a tense. Some genres are normally present tense, like romance, while others are traditionally past tense, like fantasy. If you choose a different tense, you are taking a risk on your readers.

- A thesaurus is a wonderful thing—but maintain your voice throughout your work. Having a random "perused" in there when it doesn't fit the tone of the rest will only jar your readers instead of impressing them.

Step Four

Use Punctuation as Intended

First: Stuff You Should Know

Commas and Semicolons

Commas and semicolons aren't a mystery to be unraveled. They have specific uses. I've included a crash course with all of the rules below. If your sentence doesn't fit one of these situations, you do not need to use a comma or semicolon.

If you've ever wondered when to use a comma, here you go:

1. Commas separate two independent clauses joined by a coordinating conjunction (FANBOYS).

   Ex. Harvey was a great man, and Leslie was an amazing woman.

2. Commas separate items in a series.

   Ex. You need nuts, bolts, and screws.

3. Commas are used after introductory phrases of more than two words.

   Ex. By four in the afternoon, traffic is scary on the bridges.

4. Commas separate dependent clauses at the start of the sentence from the independent clause.

   Ex. Because her alarm clock was broken, she overslept and missed the bus.

5. Commas are used to set off transitional expressions.

   Ex. Ferns, for example, need less light than other plants.

6. Commas also set of parenthetical elements.

   Ex. By the way, did you see Jim today?

7. Commas set off appositives (phrases which rename nouns or pronouns).

   Ex. Judy, our new pitcher, was late to the playoff game.

8. One word appositives are not set off when they are essential to the meaning of the sentence.

   Ex. The poet Shelly wrote "Ode to the West Wind." The poet's wife, Mary, wrote *Frankenstein*.

9. Commas are used with nonrestrictive relative clauses (clauses that start with who, which, or that that are not necessary to the meaning of the sentence).

   Ex. Raj, who is a part-time aviator, loves to tinker with machines of all kinds.

10. Commas are not used with restrictive relative clauses (clauses that begin with who, which, or that that are necessary to the meaning of the sentence).

    Ex. People who do their work efficiently make good students.

11. Commas are also used between the elements of an address.

    Ex. Send payment to 300 West Road, Stanford, CT 06860.

12. Commas also separate the elements of a date.

    Ex. The wedding is December 12, 2004.

13. Do not use a comma with a single-word address or date preceded by a preposition.

    Ex. He arrived from Baltimore in January and stayed awhile.

14. Commas are used after answering a question with *yes* or *no*.

    Ex. No, I do not like this.

15. Commas are used when addressing someone specific.

    Ex. Annie, where did you get your gun?

16. Commas are needed after interjections like ah, oh, etc.

    Ex. Ah, this water is refreshing.

17. Commas are also used to contrast.

    Ex. Harold, not Roy, is my favorite player.

If you've ever wondered when to use a semicolon, see the rules below:

1. Use a semicolon to connect two complete sentences that contain closely related ideas.
   Ex. The concert was brilliant; the crowd gave the band a standing ovation.

   Ex. I said I'd do it; I didn't say when I'd do it.

2. Use a semicolon to separate a series of items if the items are long or if they contain commas.

   Ex. The *Millenium Falcon* blasted out of Mos Eisley with Obi-Wan Kenobi, the Jedi Master; Luke Skywalker, the untried farm boy; Han Solo, the scoundrel; and Chewbacca, the hairy co-pilot on board.

3. Use a semicolon to separate two complete sentences joined with transitional phrases (on the other hand, in fact, for example).

Ex. The Force only works on the weak minded; for example, the stormtroopers whom Obi-Wan tricks into thinking their droids weren't the ones they were looking for are easily fooled.

4. Use a semicolon to separate two complete sentences joined with conjunctive adverbs such as also, anyway, finally, hence, however, instead, next, therefore, and thus.

    Ex. The cantina was filled with alien life forms; however, the two droids were not allowed inside.

Too confusing? Here's the short version:

1. Use a comma for lists of more than three items.

    a.   I made a list, checked it twice, and decided I was nice.

2. Use a comma between two complete sentences joined by any of these words: for, and, nor, but, or yet, so.

    a.   I made the nice list, and I am sure Santa would agree.

    b.   Evelyn was thrilled to see presents under the tree, but her favorite gift was playing in the snow.

3. Use a comma if you have started a sentence with words that don't contain the subject (the thing doing the action), put a comma before the subject.

    a.   Because I enjoy the winter, Christmas is my favorite holiday.

    b.   Yes, I will be traveling this holiday season.

4. If you can remove the words and not change the meaning of the sentence, put them inside commas (yes, on both sides—one before the first word and one after the last word).

    a.   I will, of course, happily join your writer's group.

    b.   John, one of my favorite writers, publishes a new book every six months.

Bottom line: don't use a comma or semicolon unless you need it!

Hyphens vs Dashes (and Parentheses)

A hyphen is what you get when you hit the button once. Hyphens go in between words like mother-in-law, joint last names like Catherine Zeta-Jones, and between adjectives before nouns like well-made suit (but not if the suit is well made! English is awesome.).

An em dash is formed when you hit the button twice (without spaces on either side) and is used to stop the flow of the sentence and demand the reader pay attention to the next detail—like this! If you want to emphasize something—put an em dash before it (and if you don't want to emphasize something, but still want to add it, use parentheses). Parentheses whisper to the readers (you can read this if you want, but you don't have to). You should not capitalize the word after the dash or beginning the parentheses; it's still a part of the same sentence and idea. You can also use a colon to introduce new information: it's a formal way to introduce something else (but it should always be either a complete sentence or a list after the colon).

- Em dashes are the result of two hyphens stuck together—they are the traditional dash in fiction. (They're the size of the letter m!)

- En dashes are slightly smaller and can be found between spans of dates (they're the size of the letter n!)

Apostrophes

Buckle up because we're doing this. Apostrophes show three things: possession, contractions, and weirdness.

Possession

1. If the word is single and doesn't end in S, put 's on the end: John's house. Meredith's horse. Bob's car.

2. If the word is single and ends in S, put either 's or ' on the end—whatever makes it easier to pronounce: Chris's house. Odysseus' crew.

3. Generally, we can do three S sounds; beyond that, it gets too messy. Say Chris's house (CHRIS-SUS HOUSE). Now say Odysseus' crew (OH-DIS-EE-US CREW). You can say Odysseus's crew, but it starts getting weird (OH-DIS-EE-US-ES CREW). Some style guides (MLA, APA, etc.) have guidelines for this, so if it matters for your situation, look it up.

4. If the word is plural and doesn't end in S, add 's: children's room. Women's restroom.

5. If the word is plural and ends in S, add ': Drivers' garages. Sharks' enclosure.

Contractions

You know this one. If you don't want to say all of the letters, use an apostrophe to show where you left some out. Don't. Can't. Won't.

Make sure that your apostrophe/single quote is facing the right direction.

- To shorten the 1960s, you should say the '60s, not the '60s. (Yes, you can also write the '60's or 1960's—just be consistent with whatever format you use.)

- If you shorten a word like until, it should be 'til (not 'til).

- If someone says 'em instead of them, make sure the single quotation mark/apostrophe is facing where the missing letters would be.

Note: There's is sometimes informally understood to mean "there is" but There're isn't "There are" (even though we may say it this way).

Weirdness

If you need to show something odd, an apostrophe may help! Weird plurals like 1800's (or 1800s—just be consistent) or A's (You got all A's this semester!). Note: Other letter grades do not get apostrophes when made plural (All Bs, Cs, Ds, and Fs can wait for next semester.) Your 8's look like F's (if you're observing handwriting quirks).

Step Four Homework

1. Go through your document for each piece of punctuation and ask yourself why it is there (commas, semicolons, colons, hyphens, dashes, apostrophes). Have you used it properly? Not sure? Google is an amazing resource—no doubt someone has already answered your question online (and probably made a video about it too!).

2. Keep a running list of problem sentences or areas that you need to work on. Keep this in a separate area from your style issues—punctuation is a mechanical matter. Yes, there are stylistic options, but for the most part, it's either right or wrong.

3. Challenge yourself: The internet is filled with practice exercises for punctuation. Don't rely on Grammarly to find your errors—go out and hone your craft. Take some online quizzes; revise some practice sentences. Teach yourself how to use these marks appropriately. Punctuation isn't the main tool in your arsenal as a writer—but it is one of your most used tools. Learn to use it properly!

EXTRA! EXTRA!
While we're here…

- Avoid comma abuse! If it's not on the list as a reason, don't use it.

  ○ Don't put commas between subjects and verbs.

  ○ Don't put commas between complete sentences.

- The Oxford Comma matters. That is all (except it isn't … because here I go: <start rant>).

  ○ The Oxford Comma is the comma before the "and" in a list of three or more items. Here's why it matters:

    ▪ We invited the strippers, JFK, and Stalin to the party.

      ▫ Epic party! You have three attendees—strippers, JFK, and Stalin.

    ▪ We invited the strippers, JFK and Stalin.

      ▫ Umm… JFK and Stalin are the strippers? Yes. When you don't have a second comma, whatever comes after the first comma is an example of the first thing you listed.

- "Who's" means "who is." If you can't replace it with "who is," you need "whose."

  ○ Who's at the door?

  ○ Whose house is this?

- Who and whom (for whom it concerns): who is subjective, the subject or actor in the sentence (can be replaced with she or he or they); whom is objective, the receiver of the sentence's action (can be replaced with her or him or them). "Who" always does things to "whom." "Whom" has things done to it.

Step Five

Track Your Bad Habits

<u>First, Stuff You Should Know</u>

You already know this. All writers have bad habits—even your editors! We overcome these pests by keeping track of them so that we can find (and fix) them next time. Start a Bad Habit Log (online, on paper, whatever works for you). Organize it into several sections:

- Punctuation you misuse (and how you plan to learn to use it properly)

- Misused words (keep a running list of confusing words—you'll learn them eventually! Or you will learn to avoid them. I have a Ph.D. in English and I still can't keep "past" and "passed" straight without looking it up—I rewrite the sentence instead.)

- Sentence structure issues (we will cover this in steps 6 and 7)

- Repeated words (We all have them. My characters are always nodding and shrugging. I make a point of searching just for those words and replacing them—and my editor still finds too many!)

Step Five Homework

Start your Bad Habit Log (which will eventually become your Become-a-Better-Writer Handbook).

1. Take note of any punctuation that confuses you. Have questions about how to use something? Jot them down in the log and research them later. Don't lose editing momentum in the middle of something. Keep working until you need a break—then go look up any questions you had.

2. Start a running log of words that mess with you and their meaning. Writing things down helps you remember them, so the act of recording this should start the process!

3. CTRL F (Command F on a Mac) for the following words: nod, shrug, laugh, sigh, said, look, felt, realize, knew, experience, heard, or anything else that you know you use too often. Log the troublesome words/phrases—and replace them with something more effective.

Part Three

Come over to the Deep
End—you'll be fine!

Step Six

7 Tweak Your Sentence Structure

First, Stuff You Should Know

Sentence structure refers to the way your sentences are designed. Generally speaking, English is an SVO/C language, meaning that readers expect the order to be Subject (the actor or doer in the sentence), Verb (the action in the sentence), and then Object (the thing affected by the verb's action) or Complement (a word that refers back to the subject).

For example, in this sentence "John drove the car," "John" is the subject, "drove" is the verb, and "car" is the object. If you rearrange the word order, you lose the meaning (Car drove the John? That's creepy.) For another example, in this sentence "John is wonderful," "John" is still the subject, "is" is the verb, and "wonderful" is the subject complement (a noun or adjective that complements or renames the subject).

You can play with this order for effect, but flipping word order turns you into Yoda (and at some point, lose your readers you will!). Writers stumble into some common errors with structure, so let's tackle those now.

Modifiers

> "I once shot an elephant in my pajamas. How he got in my pajamas I'll never know." –Groucho Marx

A modifier is any word in your sentence that gives extra information. Modifiers don't perform any grammatical function (they aren't subjects, verbs, objects, or complements). These are the people who show up to help you move, eat your pizza, drink your beer, and generally make the process more fun—but they will not pivot your couch or lift your dresser. Modifiers give details or specifics to enhance the communication. Common modifiers are adjectives (words that describe nouns), adverbs (words that describe verbs), and prepositional phrases (which act as both adjectives and adverbs—but get really clunky if you have a lot of them!). Because English relies so heavily on syntax, or word order, modifiers lose their meaning if they are not properly placed in the sentence. A few common modifier issues are a misplaced modifier, a squinting/ambiguous modifier, and a dangling modifier.

1. Misplaced Modifier: Modifiers need to be next to the word they modify—otherwise, things get weird.

   - We passed a moose driving a car through the forest.
     - Wait—what? The moose is driving the car? No—we are driving the car. The modifier phrase (driving a car through the woods) is in the wrong spot. We need to say: While driving the car through the woods, we passed a moose.
   - John served the turkey to the guests covered in gravy.
     - That sounds like a messy dinner! The modifier (covered in gravy) needs to be next to the turkey—not the guests. We should say: John served the turkey covered in gravy to the guests.
   - This is also true for one-word modifiers like just, almost, nearly, and only. These words modify the word that follows them, so be careful where you put them! There is a huge difference

between "I won almost $100" ($99.95?) and "I almost won $100" (Nope—better luck next time)!

2. Squinting/Ambiguous Modifier: Modifiers that could apply to either the previous word or the following word are considered squinting (because they are "looking" in both directions).

- People who date online frequently share horror stories.
    - Is it frequent online daters who share stories? Or do online daters often share stories? I can't tell because "frequently" is squinting/ambiguous.

- People who dine out often find themselves broke before payday.
    - People who often eat out are broke? Or people who eat out are often broke?

3. Dangling Modifier: Modifiers that refer to something that isn't even in the sentence are called dangling modifiers. They leave readers hanging, waiting for the thing to modify, but they never actually get anything.

- During childhood, my father was never around.
    - According to this sentence, your father wasn't around during his own childhood.
    - "During childhood" refers to the speaker—but the speaker (I) is never mentioned in the sentence. This sentence can be fixed in multiple ways:
        - During childhood, I missed my absent father ("During childhood" clearly modifies I here).
        - During my childhood, my father wasn't around. (In this case, the phrase "during my childhood" tells me when your father wasn't around, and if you tell me when something happens, you're an adverb—so the modifier is attached to the right piece of information.

- As a baby, my mother insists I never slept through the night.

  ○ So, your mother is insisting this when she was a baby? No, you are the baby.

  ○ Revise: According to my mother, I never slept through the night as a baby. Or: My mother recounts how I never slept through the night as a baby.

- Note: When you begin a sentence with an introductory phrase (a phrase before the subject of the sentence), the word or phrase that comes after the first comma is what those first few words refer to.

  ○ After the movie, the beach was a lovely place to visit. Ack! The beach went to the movies? No—you need someone/something to do the thing after the movie. Or rearrange the sentence without the intro phrase: The beach was a lovely place to visit after the movie.

  ○ Standing in line, the luggage just kept piling up in front of the frustrated father. So, the luggage is standing in line? No—the father is standing in line: Standing in line, the frustrated father eyed the growing pile of luggage.

4. Limiting Modifiers: Limiting modifiers get their name because they specify conditions that restrict the word they are modifying. This error often occurs with words like "only," "just," and "almost." These words move forward in the sentence, modifying the word that comes after them.

   - My sister **only** eats the green candies. As the sentence stands, it states that the writer's sister eats nothing else but green candies (no meat, no dairy, no vegetables--just green candy). Similar to misplaced modifiers, you can edit this error by moving the modifier closer to the word it should be modifying: My sister eats **only** the green candies.

Parallelism

Readers expect sentences to match in format—and when they don't, it's jarring.

- Consider this sentence: I went to the store, shopping, and eat pizza. Ouch! My brain doesn't know what to do with that! This sentence isn't parallel in verb tense. It can be:

  ○ I went to the store, shopped for new clothes, and ate with some friends.

  ○ I will go to the store, shop for clothes, and eat with my friends.

  ○ I am going to the store, shopping for new clothes, and eating with my friends.

    ▪ Any one of those works—but the pattern of the words in a single sentence need to match (or it will just feel weird to the reader—like a car with a bad shimmy).

- Parallelism occurs with verb tense, as above, but also with prepositional phrases (if you have one in a list, you need each item to have one too) and even clauses.

  ○ Consider this sentence: I like to read stories with characters who fall instantly in love, overcome challenges together as a team, and live happily ever after at the end. It has a standard intro: Subject/I + verb/like + object/to read stories + PP/with characters. Then we get into the parallel bits in clause format (clause is a fancy word for a group words that include a subject and a verb). This clause includes a subject/who followed by verbs (fall/overcome/ live), adverbs (instantly/together/happily) and a prepositional phrase (in love/as a team/at the end). Each part of the sentence repeats, using the same type of words in the same order. Check your longer sentences for parallel elements.

- If you stumble while reading them out loud, that's a good sign that some element isn't matching the rest of the format.

Step Six Homework

1. Check your document for modifiers.

    a. Scan the start of sentences. If you have a comma after a few words, make sure that the word right after that comma is the thing that those first few words are talking about.

    b. Scan for misplaced and squinting modifiers—are the words/phrases in the right spot?

    c. CTRL F (Command F on a Mac) for limiting modifiers: almost, just, nearly, and only. Make sure they are in the right place for your intended meaning (remember Sally!).

2. While we're here, let's clean up some wordiness.

    a. CTRL F (Command F on a Mac) for really, mostly, kind of, sort of, maybe, maybe, quite, more, many, other, couple of, about, literally, moderately, and very. Is there a more concise way to say it?

        - Is he very angry? Say flustered, enraged, speechless.

        - Are there many people? Say crowd, throng, mob.

        - Is it kind of sad? Comment with tearjerker, tragic, or pathetic.

- Is it really something? Odds are one word conveys the same idea.

I just stumbled on this sentence: She removed her blade from the scabbard at her hip.

- Okay, I get it—but this is a very long-winded way to say a simple thing.

- She unsheathed her blade.

  ○ This is much shorter—and it uses the appropriate word! You can add the hip part if it matters—but honestly, where else would she keep it? On her back? That would have probably come up already.

Note: This doesn't mean you should go thesaurus-crazy and use every fancy word you find. Follow your voice and maintain your tone, but clean up extra modifiers if it fits your situation.

b. Use CTRL F (Command F on a Mac) to find the word "that." Look at each one. If you removed it, would the sentence still make sense? If the answer is yes, delete it. English speakers pad their sentences with extra *that's* everywhere!

3. Scan subjects and verbs--make sure you have complete sentences! An artful fragment here and there is nice; multiple fragments look like you don't know what you're doing.

Extra Practice for Modifiers

Revise the following sentences for modifier issues.

1. Feeling hot, our sweaters ended up on the floor.

2. Raising her hand, the question was answered by Jessica in the chat window.

3. Swimming out to sea, the current grew stronger as we got farther from shore.

4. He kept a black book of all the women he had dated in his desk.

5. A shovel was used, building the sandcastle.

Extra Practice Answers: Modifiers

Here are some possible revisions. You can fix these sentences in many ways—but they can't stay the way they are.

1. Feeling hot, we tossed our sweaters on the floor.

2. Raising her hand, Jessica answered the question in the chat window.

3. As we swam out to sea, the current strengthened.

4. Inside his desk, he kept his record of the women he previously dated.

5. The little girl used a shovel to build the sandcastle.

EXTRA! EXTRA!
While we're here…

<u>Let's Play the Only Game!</u>

The word "only" modifies the next word or phrase in the sentence. If you move it, you shift the sentence's meaning!

- **Only** <u>Harry</u> said he loved Sally. Harry was the only one who said it.

- Harry **only** <u>said</u> he loved Sally. Perhaps he didn't mean it?

- Harry said **only** <u>he</u> loved Sally. Harry is telling people that he is the only one who loves Susan.

- Harry said he **only** <u>loved</u> Sally. Does he even like her? No. Just love.

- Harry said he loved **only** <u>Sally</u>. Harry said he loved <u>Sally</u> **only**. Apparently, Sally is the only one for Harry. Note: If "only" is the final word in the sentence, it refers to the previous word or phrase.

<u>A Note on YOLO (Pet Peeve Time!)</u>

The phrase YOLO has been used as a short version of "You only live once" (an updated version of *carpe diem* or "Seize the moment!"). The users of this phrase think that this sequence of words suggests that they are living in the moment—because you only have one to live, live in the moment, seize the day, man, etc. This sentiment, however, is not what YOLO tells the listener. Think of how the word "only" works--it modifies the word after it in the sentence.

- You **only** <u>live</u> once. This sentence says that the only thing you will do once in your life is live. Everything else in life, you must do twice. Skydiving? Do it again. Awful breakup? Twice. YOLO tattoo? Get two of them.

- For YOLO to mean *carpe diem*, it should be YLOO= You Live Only Once. I know—not nearly as catchy—but more accurate.

Step Seven

Add Sentence Variety

First, Stuff You Should Know

Gary Provost gives this example:

> This sentence has five words. Here are five more words. Five-word sentences are fine. But several together become monotonous. Listen to what is happening. The writing is getting boring. The sound of it drones. It's like a stuck record. The ear demands some variety. Now listen. I vary the sentence length, and I create music. Music. The writing sings. It has a pleasant rhythm, a lilt, a harmony. I use short sentences. And I use sentences of medium length. And sometimes, when I am certain the reader is rested, I will engage him with a sentence of considerable length, a sentence that burns with energy and builds with all the impetus of a crescendo, the roll of the drums, the crash of the cymbals—sounds that say listen to this, it is important.

Look at the length of the sentences here. Some are short—even one word; some are medium (10-ish words); one is a beast—but well worth the effort. Your readers appreciate variety in length and structure.

Step Seven Homework

1. Scan each paragraph in your document for the following:

    a. Sentences that start with the same word—Is it all I, I, I, or He, he, he? Edit for some variety—add a prepositional phrase or an introductory clause to shake it up. You can have two sentences of the same structure, but a few in a row makes for tedious reading.

    b. Sentences that start with the same construction—is every first word ___ing? Reaching for his coat, he turned to leave. Standing in the doorway, he looked over his shoulder. Tears shining in his eyes, he nodded once. I want to follow the scene here (clearly some emotions happening!), but I'm so distracted by the same structure for every sentence!

    c. Look from capital letter to end punctuation. How long are your sentences? Is there a variety within paragraphs? If not, switch it up some!

2. Review the start of each chapter. Does every chapter begin the same way—character's name, dialogue, The? Change it up!

Intense Homework Session (for the Super Dedicated)

Underline the subject and verb of each sentence in your document. Start from the last sentence and work backward, reading each sentence in isolation that way (this also helps you catch errors and weirdness because you're not reading the story—just the words).

- Example: "I decided to walk home before dark" or "Upon finding myself in the midst of a canyon in which there were many geese, I decided to walk home before dark."

- Simple sentences = subject + verb + object ("I ate food"). How many sentences out of the total number of sentences begin with a simple subject/verb construction (where sentence starts with subject and verb: "I was," "she walked," "he ran")? Change it up so you have some variety!

Part Four

Before you click "Send"…

Step Eight

Know What You Want

First, Stuff You Should Know

Editors are not all the same. We focus on different things, specialize in certain areas, and tweak for specific issues. Here's a brief overview of some varieties of editing.

First, some terms to clarify: proofreading, copyediting, and editing.

Proofreaders fix surface-level issues to make the sentences grammatically correct (spelling, punctuation, and basic sentence structure—maybe). They do not make your words shiny or impressive or even more effective—they simply bring them up to code. Proofreading typically occurs after your manuscript has been accepted, edited, and even typeset—proofreaders scan for last-minute typos and errors one last time before sending your work out the door to face the public.

Copyeditors and editors generally perform the same service, but pay attention to the title of the service offered. What does the editor call her services? (Note: Copywriters create text for advertisements and marketing materials. Some of them also edit on the side, but copywriting ability does not automatically mean editing skills). They fix the errors in your writing, but they also rework sentences to show their best side to readers. A good editor will whip your prose into shape without losing your narrative voice in the process (it's still you—but dressed to impress with your perfect hair and shiny smile!).

Editing Levels

Most editors will offer a wide selection of services for a variety of prices. Do some research online to make sure your potential editor is within the suggested price points for services and that you understand what they will be doing for that price point.

- Developmental Editing—This service provides feedback on your idea/outline/concept/really rough draft. This process does not adjust for sentence structure, focusing on the story and world as a whole to evaluate how well it works for readers (so far). This editing should be done before any line editing or copyediting (Why polish sentences that may not make it into the final version?).

- Line Editing—This service focuses on your work line by line, tweaking your words so the sentences are stronger. Most line edits will fix basic grammar in the process (run-on sentences, obvious misspellings), but the focus will be on strengthening each sentence to pack the most punch. Editors will note repeated words and phrases (perhaps sending your document back with all 1147 extra *That's* highlighted in yellow), drawing your attention to your bad habits so you can improve as a writer. Editors will smooth tone and narrative pacing in the process, tightening dialogue and cutting out any slack. Editors will comment on confusing scenes (and may or may not fix them for you). If you want to improve your writing style with feedback and tips, line editing is for you. Editors will leave usually comments throughout that promote your growth as a writer.

- Copyediting—This service focuses on grammatical issues, bringing everything up to code (and sometimes above). Copyeditors may provide a style sheet with explanations of common issues for you to review afterward. Copyeditors will also pay attention to continuity—both in story (characters, place, setting, etc.) and format (hyphens, capitalizations, spelling, etc.). If you just want someone to fix your stuff and call it done without much feedback (beyond a style sheet), copyediting is for you.

- ○ Yes, one person can provide both copyediting and line editing—but you have to say that is what you want.

- Format Editing—If you are writing non-fiction or academic work, you may need help with formatting according to specific style guides (MLA, APA, Chicago, etc.). Format editors ensure that your document adheres to the newest requirements for that style. They do not provide feedback on *what* is said (unless you ask for that—and it's extra!); the focus is on citations, headings, and some sentence structure issues (APA requires specific tenses in certain situations; MLA has rules for person usage, etc.).

Pricing

Editors charge by the hour or by word count/page. Be clear about which method your editor uses—and what is meant by each one. The Editorial Freelancers association is a great resource when considering standard rates.

For example, I generally charge $5 per page for line editing (my page is roughly 300 words in Times New Roman 12-point font, double-spaced—no quadruple spaces between paragraphs). I look at the entire document and round down (so 96 double-spaced pages/26,936 words would get rounded down for front matter and chapter spaces to 90 pages—$450). To edit the same piece for formatting, assuming the references fill about 12-15 pages—pretty standard for a thesis or some dissertations—it's much cheaper: only $3 page for APA ($270) or $2 page for MLA ($180). MLA has far fewer restrictions on tense—APA format means I have to read every verb; MLA means I skim for sources and headings.

Because I charge by page and not by time, you know the total cost upfront. Editors who charge by hour may present their fees differently

(I would be very careful about expectations here). Note: if you are using an hourly editor, ask what programs they use, if any. I don't use any automated programs to help me edit (I'm a luddite this way; no judgment—I just don't like them), so my hourly rates would be much higher than someone who uses a program to help.

It's critical to lay out your expectations with your editor. Explain exactly what you want and get a description of the provided service in writing.

To finish my example (and shamelessly self-promote), I also accept a deposit upfront ($50-$100) and the rest on delivery. I generally send an email overview with an overall response along with the edited manuscript (I use Word's Track Changes so you can see everything).

Editors work in different ways—ask how yours operates before agreeing to anything! Communication is key!

Step Eight Homework

1. Decide what you need—developmental, line edits, copyediting, format help. Research how much your needs will cost you. Editing can be expensive—but it can make or break a book. (Note: Beware any editor who claims they can make your work a best seller. We can't. But we can improve your chances of success by polishing your prose to the highest sheen! Readers prefer well-written books.).

2. Find some possible editors. Do your research—look people up online! Read reviews. Take fellow authors' recommendations. Be careful out there.

3. When you find someone you like who does what you want, ask for samples of previous work to see if their style meshes with your expectations. Some editors will have you send a few pages of the work in question to get a sense of what they can do.

4. Get a detailed explanation of cost, timeframe, and process. Know what you are getting into. Will the editor communicate with you during the process? Do you want to meet with them before, during, or after the edits, and is your editor willing?

5. Have an agreement in writing. No, you don't need your lawyer to draft a contract—but you can. Do not rely on a phone conversation alone.

Step Nine

Create a Style Sheet
for Your Work

First, Stuff You Should Know

Every single book is different. Character quirks, town names, weapon titles, positions of authority—everything is formatted according to your design (within reason—English has some rules and expectations).

- Have a character who doesn't use contractions? Let your editor know on the style sheet.

- Have a magic weapon named The Cursed Mistress? Is "The" part of the title? Let the editor know!

- Have a special social class that's a foreign word to your main characters? Let your editor know to put in italics.

- Use a special magic word that's always lowercase? Tell your editor.

Your style sheet should include anything specific to this work (or world) that isn't self-explanatory. For instance, editors know to capitalize character names; editors don't know whether you capitalize the nickname *chaivin* (Is it like babe or honey? Or more like *Sassenach*?).

Step Nine Homework

1. Create a style sheet for your work. Include any quirks that the editor needs to know. Have this ready to send with your manuscript.

2. This does not need to be a mini-book! You may decide to create an entire guidebook for your world/series, but this need not detail each character's lineage. This is about specific words and how you want them to look in the final version. Your style sheet should be 1-3 pages.

3. If your book doesn't have any quirks, then ignore this step! But while you're here, you might as well learn something.

Step Ten

Just Breathe. You Can Do This. I Promise.

<u>Stuff You Already Know</u>

You made it! Take a moment and soak in this feeling of accomplishment.

It was a slog, but you persevered! I promise that next time around, this process will be slightly easier (just a smidge). By book ten, this will be familiar (still taxing, but not nearly as scary). You will start to incorporate better habits as you write, so you don't have to tweak them later.

Editing your own work provides a sense of pride, and while a professional is always going to do more (they should—it's their job!), doing some of the legwork on your own empowers you as a writer, granting you agency and confidence. You know you can tell a story—now learn how to dress it in the best clothes and brush its hair! One way to become a better writer is to write, and the same applies to editing your own work—practice, practice, practice! The knowledge will come.

Final Thoughts/Tips

1. Read. Read in your genre. Read outside of your comfort zone. Read established writers with distinctive voices. Read emerging writers with astounding vision.

2. Learn the rules. You can't effectively break the rules of grammar without knowing them (otherwise your clever fragment may just look like a mistake!). Take it slow, but take the idea of learning to wield your tools, your words, seriously. Tons of books, blogs, and videos cover the rules. Check them out! I'm a fan of the classic *Eats, Shoots, & Leaves: The Zero Tolerance Approach to Punctuation* by Lynn Trusse. I also recommend *Woe is I: The Grammarphobe's Guide to Better English in Plain English* by Patricia T. O'Conner.

3. Read your work out loud ... backward. Yes, I said backward. Start with the final sentence, find the capital letter that starts it, and read that sucker aloud to the end punctuation (period, question mark, exclamation mark). Is it a complete thought? Does it make sense? Cool. Go back or up a line. Find the previous sentence and repeat the process. Reading your sentences in isolation forces you to look at them one by one (instead of the way you read the story). You likely won't do this for the entire thing, but you can put a serious dent in troublesome areas this way.

    a. Live with someone? Or have a very expressive pet? Read your story out loud and watch their reaction. If their expression is confused, mark that spot to revise later. If you stumble, mark that part to revise later. You're not narrating here (though I suppose you could if you're supper confident in your splicing skills); you're reading for flow and comprehension.

4. Take breaks. Editing is not a one-and-done event. It can be a marathon of late nights, early mornings, and five-minute breaks from work (and lots of tea if you're me!). It's best accomplished in small chunks with a specific focus. If you read your work straight through looking for all of the things, you will find some of the problem stuff—but definitely not everything (not without making yourself crazy first!).

5. At some point, your manuscript is finished. Let it go. Yes, you could make it better tomorrow—but how many tomorrows are spent re-working something when you could be on to your next story? Academics say papers are never done—just due. Give yourself a deadline and stick to it. Find your "good enough" point and watch *Frozen* (Let it go!!!). We will never get to see it if you keep tinkering with chapter five.

6. Remember that your story is worth telling. No one can tell it like you can. No one else can do what you can. Don't give up. We need to read your words. Get it out in the world!

Author Bio

D r. Jenifer Paquette teaches English in higher education with her areas of expertise running from the history of the English language and the intricacies of grammatical rules to guidelines for effective writing and communication across disciplines. When she isn't grading essays or editing manuscripts for academics and creative writers, JM Paquette spends her time writing fantasy and paranormal romance novels. She can be found at authorjmpaquette.com and 4horsemenpublications.com and as Author JM Paquette on Facebook and Instagram.